# Lily's African Adventure

## The Quest for the Hidden Treasure

All rights are reserved Safari Scribe. 2023
part of this publication may be reproduced, stored in a retr al system or transmitted in any form or by any means, electron mechanical, photocopying, recording or otherwise, withou prior permission.

Join Lily, a brave and curious adventurer, as she embarks on an exciting journey through the stunning landscapes of Africa in pursuit of a hidden treasure. Along the way, she encounters magnificent wildlife, overcomes numerous challenges, and discovers valuable lessons about bravery, compassion, and self-discovery. "Lily's African Adventure: The Quest for the Hidden Treasure" is an enchanting tale that encourages young readers to believe in their potential and the magic of their dreams. This captivating story is perfect for young explorers aged 5-7, and will definitely leave a lasting impression. So come and join Lily on her unforgettable quest, and discover the true treasure that lies within!

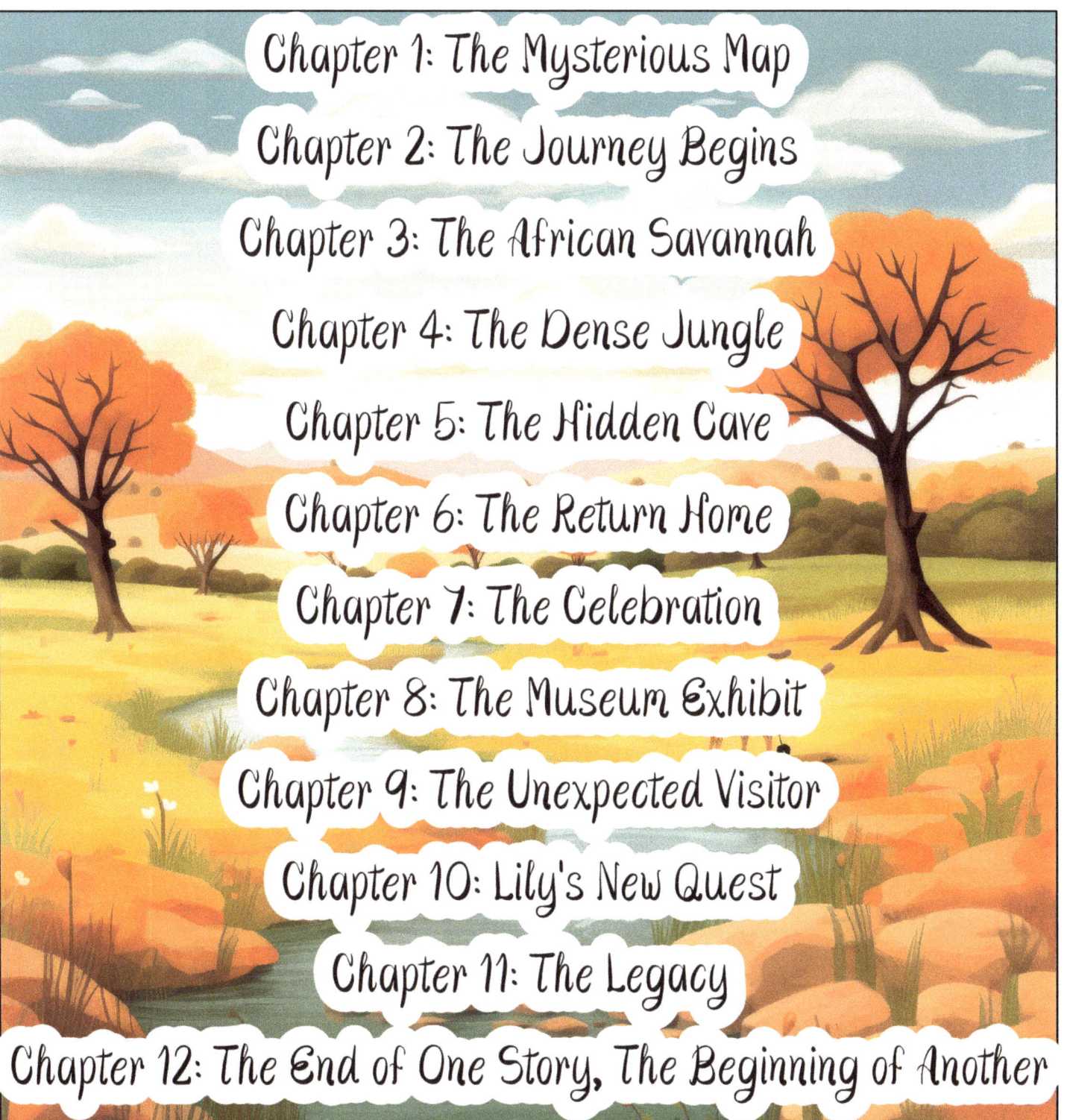

# The Mysterious Map

Once upon a time, in a small town named Harmonyville, lived a bright and curious girl named Lily. Lily was known for her adventurous spirit and her love for stories about lost treasures. One day, she found an old, dusty map in her grandmother's attic. The map was beautifully drawn and showed a path leading to a hidden treasure in the heart of Africa. Lily's heart raced with excitement. She knew she had to find this treasure.

# The Journey Begins

With her parents' permission, Lily embarked on her journey. She packed her backpack with essentials and held the map close to her heart. She boarded a plane to Africa, her heart filled with anticipation and excitement. As she looked out of the window, she saw the vast African landscape, a mix of golden savannahs and dense forests. She knew her adventure had just begun.

# The African Savannah

Lily's first stop was the African savannah. She saw herds of elephants, prides of lions, and flocks of colorful birds. She met a wise old elephant named Bantu who told her that the treasure she seeks requires courage, determination, and a kind heart. Lily thanked Bantu and promised to remember his words. She then continued her journey, her mind set on finding the treasure.

# The Dense Jungle

Next, Lily had to cross a dense jungle. It was challenging, with thick vegetation and unknown sounds. But Lily was determined. She remembered Bantu's words and pushed forward. She helped a trapped baby monkey get free and in return, the monkey showed her a shortcut through the jungle. Lily realized that kindness was indeed a treasure

# The Hidden Cave

Finally, Lily reached a hidden cave where the map indicated the treasure would be. It was dark and scary, but Lily was brave. She ventured inside and found a beautiful chest. As she opened it, she found it filled with gold, jewels, and ancient artifacts. But among them, she found a small mirror. As she looked into it, she saw her own reflection — a brave, kind, and determined girl. She realized that she was the real treasure

# The Return Home

Lily returned home, her heart full of joy and her mind full of memories. She had found the treasure, but more importantly, she had discovered her own strength and kindness. She had achieved what she had set her mind on. From then on, Lily knew that she could accomplish anything she put her mind to. And so, her African adventure ended, but her journey of self-discovery had just begun.

# The Celebration

Upon Lily's return, the whole town of Harmonyville was waiting to celebrate her successful adventure. They were all eager to hear about her journey. Lily shared her experiences, the friends she made, and the lessons she learned. The townsfolk listened in awe, their eyes sparkling with admiration for the brave and kind-hearted girl.

# The Museum Exhibit

Lily decided to donate the treasure she found to the local museum, so everyone could learn about the rich history and culture it represented. The museum set up an exhibit called "Lily's African Adventure," which included the map, the treasure, and pictures of her journey. It quickly became the most popular exhibit, inspiring other children to learn more about different cultures and the value of bravery and kindness.

# Lily's New Quest

Inspired by her adventure, Lily decided to start a new quest. She started a club in her school called "The Adventurer's Guild." The club was dedicated to learning about different cultures, going on local adventures, and helping those in need. Lily's adventure had sparked a sense of curiosity and kindness among the children of Harmonyville.

# The Legacy

Years passed, and Lily grew up to be a renowned explorer and a kind-hearted leader. Her story became a legend in Harmonyville. The map and the mirror from the treasure chest were passed down as heirlooms, reminding everyone of Lily's adventure and the lessons she learned. Her legacy was not just about the treasure she found, but the values of courage, determination, and kindness she embodied.

## The End of One Story, The Beginning of Another

As Lily looked back at her life, she realized that her African adventure was just the beginning. It was the start of a journey that led her to discover her own strength, to inspire others, and to leave a lasting legacy. She smiled, knowing that she had indeed achieved what she had set her mind on. And with that, she prepared for another adventure, ready to discover new treasures and learn new lessons.

Thank you for purchasing my book! I hope it brings you joy and relaxation.

I would greatly appreciate your feedback on your experience with the book. Your comments will help me improve future editions and provide the best possible coloring experience for others.

Thank you again for your support!

www.ingramcontent.com/pod-product-compliance
Lightning Source LLC
LaVergne TN
LVHW070222080526
838202LV00068B/6886